P9-AGQ-797

Encyclical Letter of
Pope Leo XIII

THE
RESTORATION
OF CHRISTIAN
PHILOSOPHY

Aeterni Patris

Pauline
BOOKS & MEDIA

BOSTON

Aeterni Patris originally appeared in *The Catholic World* in 1879.

ISBN 0-8198-6443-9

Printed and published by Pauline Books & Media, 50 St. Paul's Avenue, Boston, MA 02130.

Pauline Books & Media is the publishing house of the Daughters of St. Paul, an international congregation of women religious serving the Church with the communications media.

The only-begotten Son of the Eternal Father, who came on earth to bring salvation and the light of divine wisdom to men, conferred a great and wonderful blessing on the world when, about to ascend again into heaven, He commanded the apostles to go and teach all nations,[1] and left the Church which He had founded to be the common and supreme teacher of the peoples. For men, whom the truth had set free, were to be preserved by the truth; nor would the fruits of heavenly doctrines, by which salvation comes to men, have long remained had not the Lord Christ appointed an unfailing authority for the instruction of the faithful. And the Church built upon the promises of its own divine Author, whose charity it imitated, so faithfully followed out His commands that its constant aim and chief wish was this: to teach true religion and contend forever against errors. To this end assuredly have tended the incessant labors of individual bishops; to this end also the published laws and decrees of Councils, and especially the constant watchfulness of the Roman Pontiffs, to whom, as successors of the blessed Peter in the primacy of the apostles, belongs the right and office of teaching and confirming their brethren in the faith. Since, then, according to the warning of the Apostle, the minds of Christ's faithful are apt to be deceived and the integrity of the faith to be corrupted among men *by philosophy and vain deceit*,[2] the supreme pastors of the Church have always thought it their duty to advance, by every means in their power, science truly so called, and at the same time to provide with special care that all studies should accord with the Catholic faith, especially philosophy, on which a right apprehension of the other sciences in great part depends. Indeed, venerable brethren, on this very subject among others, we briefly admonished you in our first encyclical letter; but now, both by reason of the gravity of the subject and the condition of the time, we are again compelled to speak to you on the mode of taking up the study of philosophy which shall respond most fitly to the true faith, and at the same time be most consonant with the dignity of human knowledge.

Whoso turns his attention to the bitter strifes of these days and seeks a reason for the troubles that vex public and private life must come to the conclusion that a fruitful cause of the evils which now afflict, as well as of those which threaten us, lies in this: that false conclusions concerning divine and human things, which originated in the schools of philosophy, have crept into all the orders of the state, and have been accepted by the common consent of the masses. For since it is in the very nature of man to follow the guide of reason in his actions, if his intellect sins at all his will soon follows; and thus it happens that looseness of intellectual opinion influences human actions and perverts them. Whereas, on the other hand, if men be of sound mind and take their stand on true and solid principles, there will result a vast amount of benefits for the public and private good. We do not, indeed, attribute such force and authority to philosophy as to esteem it equal to the task of combating and rooting out all errors; for, when the Christian religion was first constituted, it came upon earth to restore it to its primeval dignity by the admirable light of faith, diffused not by persuasive words of human wisdom, but in the manifestation of spirit and of power[3]; so also at the present time we look above all things to the powerful help of Almighty God to bring back to a right understanding the minds of men and dispel the darkness of error. But the natural helps with which the grace of the divine wisdom, strongly and sweetly disposing all things, has supplied the human race are neither to be despised nor neglected, chief among which is evidently the right use of philosophy. For not in vain did God set the light of reason in the human mind; and so far is the super-added light of faith from extinguishing or lessening the power of the intelligence that it completes it rather, and by adding to its strength renders it capable of greater things.

Therefore divine Providence itself requires that in calling back the peoples to the paths of faith and salvation, advantage should be taken of human science also—an approved and wise practice which history testifies was observed by the most illustrious Fathers of the Church. They, indeed, were wont neither to belittle nor undervalue the part that reason had to play, as is summed up by the great Augustine when he attributes to this science "that by which the most wholesome faith is begotten,…is nourished, defended, and made strong."[4]

In the first place, philosophy, if rightly made use of by the wise, in a certain way tends to smooth and fortify the road to true faith, and to prepare the souls of its disciples for the fit reception of revelation; for which reason it is well called by ancient writers sometimes a stepping-stone to the Christian faith,[5] sometimes the prelude and help of Christianity,[6] sometimes the Gospel teacher.[7] And assuredly the God of all goodness, in all that pertains to divine things, has not only manifested by the light of faith those truths which human intelligence could not attain of itself, but others also not altogether unattainable by reason, that by the help of divine authority they may be made known to all at once and without any admixture of error. Hence it is that certain truths which were either divinely proposed for belief, or were bound by the closest chains to the doctrine of faith, were discovered by pagan sages with nothing but their natural reason to guide them, were demonstrated and proved by becoming arguments. *For,* as the Apostle says, *the invisible things of him, from the creation of the world, are clearly seen, being understood by the things that are made: his eternal power also and divinity*[8]; and the Gentiles who have not the law show, nevertheless, the work of the law written in their hearts.[9] But it is most fitting to turn these truths, which have been discovered by the pagan sages even, to the use and purposes of revealed doctrine, in order to show that both human wisdom and the very testimony of our adversaries serve to support the Christian faith—a method which is not of recent introduction, but of established use, and has often been adopted by the holy Fathers of the Church. For instance, those venerable men, the witnesses and guardians of religious traditions, recognize a certain form and figure of this in the action of the Hebrews, who, when about to depart out of Egypt, were commanded to take with them the gold and silver vessels and precious robes of the Egyptians, that by a change of use the things might be dedicated to the service of the true God which had formerly been the instruments of ignoble and superstitious rites. Gregory of Neocaesarea[10] praises Origen expressly because, with singular dexterity, as one snatches weapons from the enemy, he turned to the defense of

Christian wisdom and to the destruction of superstition many arguments drawn from the writings of the pagans. And both Gregory of Nazianzus[11] and Gregory of Nyssa[12] praise and commend a like mode of disputation in Basil the Great; while Jerome especially commends it in Quadratus, a disciple of the apostles, in Aristides, Justin, Irenaeus, and very many others.[13] Augustine says: "Do we not see Cyprian, that mildest of doctors and most blessed of martyrs, going out of Egypt laden with gold and silver and vestments? And Lactantius also and Victorinus, Optatus and Hilary? And, not to speak of the living, how many Greeks have done likewise?"[14] But if natural reason first sowed this rich field of doctrine before it was rendered fruitful by the power of Christ, it must assuredly become more prolific after the grace of the Savior has renewed and added to the native faculties of the human mind. And who does not see that a plain and easy road is opened up to faith by such a method of philosophic study?

But the advantage to be derived from such a school of philosophy is not to be confined within these limits. The foolishness of those men is gravely reproved in the words of divine wisdom who by these good things that are seen could not understand Him that is, neither by attending to the works could have acknowledged who was the workman.[15] In the first place, then, this great and noble fruit is gathered from human reason, that it demonstrates that God *is; for by the greatness of the beauty, and of the creature,* the *Creator of them may be seen so as to be known thereby.*[16] Again, it shows God to excel in the height of all perfections, in infinite wisdom before which nothing lies hidden, and in absolute justice which no depraved affection could possibly shake; and that God, therefore, is not only true but truth itself, which can neither deceive nor be deceived. Whence it clearly follows that human reason finds the fullest faith and authority united in the word of God. In like manner reason declares that the doctrine of the Gospel has even from its very beginning been made manifest by certain wonderful signs, the established proofs, as it were, of unshaken truth; and that all, therefore, who set faith in the Gospel do not believe rashly as though following cunningly devised fables,[17] but, by a most reasonable consent, subject their intelligence and judgment to an authority which is divine. And

6

of no less importance is it that reason most clearly sets forth that the Church instituted by Christ (as laid down in the Vatican Synod), on account of its wonderful spread, its marvelous sanctity, and its inexhaustible fecundity in all places, as well as of its Catholic unity and unshaken stability, is in itself a great and perpetual motive of belief and an irrefragable testimony of its own divine mission.[18]

Its solid foundations having been thus laid, a perpetual and varied service is further required of philosophy, in order that sacred theology may receive and assume the nature, form, and genius of a true science. For in this, the most noble of studies, it is of the greatest necessity to bind together, as it were, in one body the many and various parts of the heavenly doctrines, that, each being allotted to its own proper place and derived from its own proper principles, the whole may join together in a complete union; in order, in fine, that all and each part may be strengthened by its own and the others' invincible arguments. Nor is that more accurate or fuller knowledge of the things that are believed, and somewhat more lucid understanding, as far as it can go, of the very mysteries of faith which Augustine and the other Fathers commended and strove to reach, and which the Vatican Synod itself[19] declared to be most fruitful, to be passed over in silence or belittled. Those will certainly more fully and more easily attain that knowledge and understanding who to integrity of life and love of faith join a mind rounded and finished by philosophic studies, as the same Vatican Synod teaches that the knowledge of such sacred dogmas ought to be sought as well from analogy of the things that are naturally known as from the connection of those mysteries one with another and with the final end of man.[20]

Lastly, the duty of religiously defending the truths divinely delivered, and of resisting those who dare oppose them, pertains to philosophic pursuits. Wherefore it is the glory of philosophy to be esteemed as the bulwark of faith and the strong defense of religion. As Clement of Alexandria testifies, the doctrine of the Savior is indeed perfect in itself and wants naught, since it is the power and wisdom of God. And the assistance of Greek philosophy makes not the truth more powerful; but in as much as it weakens the contrary arguments of the sophists and repels the veiled attacks against the truth, it

7

has been fitly called the hedge and fence of the vine.[21] For as the enemies of the Catholic name, when about to attack religion, are in the habit of borrowing their weapons from the arguments of philosophers, so the defenders of sacred science draw many arguments from the store of philosophy which may serve to uphold revealed dogmas. Nor is the triumph of the Christian faith a small one in using human reason to repel powerfully and speedily the attacks of its adversaries by the hostile arms which human reason itself supplied. Which species of religious strife St. Jerome, writing to Magnus, notices as having been adopted by the Apostle of the Gentiles himself: Paul, the leader of the Christian army skillfully turns even a chance inscription into an argument for the faith; for he had learned from the true David to wrest the sword from the hands of the enemy and to cut off the head of the boastful Goliath with his own weapon.[22] Moreover, the Church herself not only urges, but even commands, Christian teachers to seek help from philosophy. For the fifth Council of the Lateran, after it had decided that "every assertion contrary to the truth of revealed faith is altogether false, for the reason that it contradicts, however slightly, the truth,"[23] advises teachers of philosophy to pay close attention to the exposition of fallacious arguments; since, as Augustine testifies, "if reason is turned against the authority of sacred Scripture, no matter how specious it may seem it errs in the likeness of truth; for true it cannot be."[24]

But in order that philosophy may be found equal to the gathering of those precious fruits which we have indicated, it behooves it above all things never to turn aside from that path which the Fathers have entered upon from a venerable antiquity, and which the Vatican Council solemnly and authoritatively approved. As it is evident that very many truths of the supernatural order which are far beyond the reach of the keenest intellect must be accepted, human reason, conscious of its own infirmity, dare not pretend to what is beyond it, nor deny those truths, nor measure them by its own standard, nor interpret them at will; but receive them rather with a full and humble faith, and esteem it the highest honor to be allowed to wait upon heavenly doctrines like a handmaid and attendant, and by God's goodness attain to them in any way whatsoever.

But in the case of such doctrines as the human intelligence may perceive, it is equally just that philosophy should make use of its own method, principles, and arguments—not indeed in such fashion as to seem rashly to withdraw from the divine authority. But since it is established that those things which become known by revelation have the force of certain truth, and that those things which war against faith war equally against right reason, the Catholic philosopher will know that he violates at once faith and the laws of reason if he accepts any conclusion which he understands to be opposed to revealed doctrine.

We know that there are some who, in their overestimate of the human faculties, maintain that as soon as man's intellect becomes subject to divine authority it falls from its native dignity, and, hampered by the yoke of this species of slavery, is much retarded and hindered in its progress towards the supreme truth and excellence. Such an idea is most false and deceptive, and its final result is to induce foolish and ungrateful men willfully to repudiate the most sublime truths, and reject the divine gift of faith, from which the fountains of all good things flow out upon civil society. For the human mind, being confined within certain limits, and those narrow enough, is exposed to many errors and is ignorant of many things; whereas the Christian faith, reposing on the authority of God, is the unfailing mistress of truth, whom whoso follows he will be neither immeshed in the snares of error nor tossed hither and thither on the waves of fluctuating opinion. Those, therefore, who to the study of philosophy unite obedience to the Christian faith are philosophers indeed; for the splendor of the divine truths, received into the mind, helps the understanding, and not only detracts in nowise from its dignity, but adds greatly to its nobility, keenness, and stability. For surely that is a worthy and most useful exercise of reason when men give their minds to disproving those things which are repugnant to faith and proving the things which conform to faith. In the first case they cut the ground from under the feet of error and expose the viciousness of the arguments on which error rests; while in the second case they make themselves masters of weighty reasons for the sound demonstration of truth and the satisfactory instruction of any reasonable person. Whoever denies that such study and practice tend to add to the resources and expand the faculties of the mind must necessarily and absurdly hold that the mind gains nothing from discriminating between the true and the false. Justly, therefore, does the Vatican Council commemorate in these words the great benefits which faith has conferred upon reason: *Faith frees and saves reason from error, and endows it with manifold knowledge.*[25] A wise man, therefore, would not accuse faith and look upon it as opposed to reason and natural truths, but would rather offer heartfelt thanks to God, and sincerely rejoice that in the density of ignorance and in the flood-tide of error, holy faith, like a friendly star, shines down upon his path and points out to him the fair gate of truth beyond all danger of wandering.

If, venerable brethren, you open the history of philosophy, you will find all we have just said proved by experience. The philosophers of old who lacked the gift of faith, yet were esteemed so wise, fell into many appalling errors. You know how often among some truths they taught false and incongruous things; what vague and doubtful opinions they held concerning the nature of the Divinity, the first origin of things, the government of the world, the divine knowledge of the future, the cause and principle of evil, the ultimate end of man, eternal beatitude, concerning virtue and vice, and other matters, a true and certain knowledge of which is most necessary to the human race; while, on the other hand, the early Fathers and Doctors of the Church, who well understood that, according to the divine plan, the restorer of human science is Christ, who is the power and the wisdom of God,[26] *and in whom are hidden all the treasures of wisdom and knowledge,*[27] took up and investigated the books of the ancient philosophers, and compared their teachings with the doctrines of revelation, and, carefully sifting them, they cherished what was true and wise in them and amended or rejected all else. For as the all-seeing God against the cruelty of tyrants raised up mighty martyrs to the defense of the Church, men prodigal of their great lives, in like manner to false philosophers and heretics He opposed men of great wisdom, to defend, even by the aid of human reason, the treasure of revealed truths. Thus from the very first ages of the Church, Catholic doctrine has encountered a multitude of most bitter adversaries, who, deriding the Christian dogmas

10

and institutions, maintained that there were many gods, that the material world never had a beginning or cause, and that the course of events was one of blind and fatal necessity, not regulated by the will of divine Providence.

But the learned men whom we call apologists speedily encountered these teachers of foolish doctrine, and, under the guidance of faith, found arguments in human wisdom also to prove that one God, who stands pre-eminent in every kind of perfection, is to be worshiped; that all things were created from nothing by His omnipotent power; that by His wisdom they flourish and serve each their own special purposes. Among these St. Justin Martyr claims the chief place. After having tried the most celebrated academies of the Greeks, he saw clearly, as he himself confesses, that he could only draw truths in their fullness from the doctrines of revelation. These he embraced with all the ardor of his soul, purged of calumny, courageously and fully defended before the Roman emperors, and reconciled with them not a few of the sayings of the Greek philosophers.

Quadratus also and Aristides, Hermias and Athenagoras, stood nobly forth in that time. Nor did Irenaeus, the invincible martyr and bishop of Lyons, win less glory in the same cause when, forcibly refuting the perverse opinions of the Orientals, the work of the Gnostics, scattered broadcast over the territories of the Roman Empire, he explained (according to Jerome) the origin of each heresy and in what philosophic source it took its rise.[28] But who knows not the disputations of Clement of Alexandria, which the same Jerome thus honorably commemorates: "What is there in them that is not learned, and what that is not of the very heart of philosophy?"[29] He himself, indeed, with marvelous versatility treated of many things of the greatest utility for preparing a history of philosophy, for the exercise of the dialectic art, and for showing the agreement between reason and faith. After him came Origen, who graced the chair of the school of Alexandria, and was most learned in the teachings of the Greeks and Orientals. He published many volumes, involving great labor, which were wonderfully adapted to explain the divine writings and illustrate the sacred dogmas; which, though, as they now stand, not altogether free from error, contain nevertheless a wealth of knowledge tending to the growth and advance of natural truths. Tertullian opposes heretics with the authority of the sacred writings; with the philosophers he changes his fence and disputes philosophically; but so learnedly and accurately did he confute them that he made bold to say, "Neither in science nor in schooling are we equals, as you imagine."[30] Arnobius, also, in his works against the pagans, and Lactantius in the divine *Institutions* especially, with equal eloquence and strength strenuously strive to move men to accept the dogmas and precepts of Catholic wisdom, not by philosophic juggling, after the fashion of the academics, but vanquishing them partly by their own arms, and partly by arguments drawn from the mutual contentions of the philosophers.[31] But the writings on the human soul, the divine attributes, and other questions of mighty moment which the great Athanasius and Chrysostom, the prince of orators, have left behind them are, by common consent, so supremely excellent that it seems scarcely anything could be added to their subtlety and fullness. And, not to cover too wide a range, we add to the number of the great men of whom mention has been made the names of Basil the Great and of the two Gregories, who, on going forth from Athens, that home of all learning, thoroughly equipped with all the harness of philosophy, turned the wealth of knowledge which each had gathered up in a course of zealous study to the work of refuting heretics and preparing Christians.

But Augustine would seem to have wrested the palm from all. Of a most powerful genius and thoroughly saturated with sacred and profane learning, with the loftiest faith and with equal knowledge, he combated most vigorously all the errors of his age. What height of philosophy did he not reach? What region of it did he not diligently explore, either in expounding the loftiest mysteries of the faith to the faithful, or defending them against the fell onslaught of adversaries, or again when, in demolishing the fables of the academics or the Manichaeans, he laid the safe foundations and sure structure of human science, or followed up the reason, origin, and causes of the evils that afflict man? How subtly he reasoned on the angels, the soul, the human mind, the will and free choice, on religion and the life of the blessed, on time and eternity, and even on the very nature of changeable bodies! Afterwards, in the East,

John Damascene, treading in the footsteps of Basil and of Gregory Nazianzen, and in the West Boethius and Anselm, following the doctrines of Augustine, added largely to the patrimony of philosophy.

Later on the doctors of the middle ages, who are called scholastics, addressed themselves to a great work—that of diligently collecting and sifting and storing up, as it were, in one place, for the use and convenience of posterity, the rich and fertile harvests of Christian learning scattered abroad in the voluminous works of the Holy Fathers. And with regard, venerable brethren, to the origin, drift, and excellence of this scholastic learning, it may be well here to speak more fully in the words of one of the wisest of our predecessors, Sixtus V: "By the divine favor of Him who alone gives the spirit of science, and wisdom, and understanding, and who through all ages, as there may be need, enriches His Church with new blessings and strengthens it with new safeguards, there was founded by our fathers, men of eminent wisdom, the scholastic theology, which two glorious doctors in particular, the angelic St. Thomas and the seraphic St. Bonaventure, illustrious teachers of this faculty,...with surpassing genius, by unwearied diligence, and at the cost of long labors and vigils, set in order and beautified, and, when skillfully arranged and clearly explained in a variety of ways, handed down to posterity.

"And, indeed, the knowledge and use of so salutary a science, which flows from the fertilizing founts of the sacred writings, the Sovereign Pontiffs, the Holy Fathers and the councils, must always be of the greatest assistance to the Church, whether with the view of really and soundly understanding and interpreting the Scriptures, or more safely and to better purpose reading and explaining the Fathers, or for exposing and refuting the various errors and heresies; and in these late days, when those dangerous times described by the Apostle are already upon us, when the blasphemers, the proud, and the seducers go from bad to worse, erring themselves and causing others to err, there is surely a very great need of confirming the dogmas of the Catholic faith and confuting heresies."

Although these words seem to bear reference solely to scholastic theology, nevertheless they may plainly be accepted as equally true of philosophy and its praises. For the noble endowments which make the scholastic theology so formidable to the enemies of truth—to wit, as the same Pontiff adds, "that ready and close coherence of cause and effect, that order and array as of a disciplined army in battle, those clear definitions and distinctions, that strength of argument and those keen discussions, by which light is distinguished from darkness, the true from the false, expose and strip naked, as it were, the falsehoods of heretics wrapped around by a cloud of subterfuges and fallacies"[32]—those noble and admirable endowments, we say, are only to be found in a right use of that philosophy which the scholastic teachers have been accustomed carefully and prudently to make use of even in theological disputations. Moreover, since it is the proper and special office of the scholastic theologians to bind together by the fastest chain human and divine science, surely the theology in which they excelled would not have gained such honor and commendation among men if they had made use of a lame and imperfect or vain philosophy.

Among the scholastic doctors, the chief and master of all towers Thomas Aquinas, who, as Cajetan observes, because "he most venerated the ancient doctors of the Church, in a certain way seems to have inherited the intellect of all."[33] The doctrines of those illustrious men, like the scattered members of a body, Thomas collected together and cemented, distributed in wonderful order, and so increased with important additions that he is rightly esteemed the special bulwark and glory of the Catholic faith. With his spirit at once humble and swift, his memory ready and tenacious, his life spotless throughout, a lover of truth for its own sake, richly endowed with human and divine science, like the sun he heated the world with the ardor of his virtues and filled it with the splendor of his teaching. Philosophy has no part which he did not touch finely at once and thoroughly; on the laws of reasoning, on God and incorporeal substances, on man and other sensible things, on human actions and their principles, he reasoned in such a manner that in him there is wanting neither a full array of questions, nor an apt disposal of the various parts, nor the
14

best method of proceeding, nor soundness of principles or strength of argument, nor clearness and elegance of style, nor a facility for explaining what is abstruse.

Moreover, the Angelic Doctor pushed his philosophic conclusions into the reasons and principles of the things which are most comprehensive and contain in their bosom, so to say, the seeds of almost infinite truths, to be unfolded in good time by later masters and with a goodly yield. And as he also used this philosophic method in the refutation of error, he won this title to distinction for himself: that single-handed he victoriously combated the errors of former times, and supplied invincible arms to put those to rout which might in after-times spring up. Again, clearly distinguishing, as is fitting, reason from faith, while happily associating the one with the other, he both preserved the rights and had regard for the dignity of each; so much so, indeed, that reason, borne on the wings of Thomas to its human height, can scarcely rise higher, while faith could scarcely expect more or stronger aids from reason than those which she has already obtained through Thomas.

For these reasons learned men, in former ages especially, of the highest repute in theology and philosophy, after mastering with infinite pains the immortal works of Thomas, gave themselves up not so much to be instructed in his angelic wisdom as to be nourished upon it. It is known that nearly all the founders and framers of laws of the religious orders commanded their associates to study and religiously adhere to the teachings of St. Thomas, fearful lest any of them should swerve even in the slightest degree from the footsteps of so great a man. To say nothing of the family of St. Dominic, which rightly claims this great teacher for its own glory, the statutes of the Benedictines, the Carmelites, the Augustinians, the Society of Jesus, and many others, all testify that they are bound by this law.

And here how pleasantly one's thoughts fly back to those celebrated schools and academies which flourished of old in Europe, to Paris, Salamanca, Alcala, to Douay, Toulouse, and Louvain, to Padua and Bologna, to Naples and Coimbra, and to many another! All know how the fame of these seats of learning grew with their years, and that their judgment, often asked in matters of grave moment, held great weight everywhere. And we know how in those great homes of human wisdom, as in his own kingdom, Thomas reigned supreme; and that the minds of all, of teachers as well as of taught, rested in wonderful harmony under the shield and authority of the Angelic Doctor.

But, furthermore, our predecessors in the Roman pontificate have celebrated the wisdom of Thomas Aquinas by exceptional tributes of praise and the most ample testimonials. Clement VI in the Bull *In Ordine,* Nicholas V in his Brief to the Friars of the Order of Preachers, 1451, Benedict XIII in the Bull *Pretiosus,* and others bear witness that the universal Church borrows luster from his admirable teaching; while St. Pius V declares in the Bull *Mirabilis* that heresies, confounded and convicted by the same teaching, were dissipated, and the whole world daily freed from fatal errors; others, such as Clement XII in the Bull *Verbo Dei,* affirm that most fruitful blessings have spread abroad from his writings over the whole Church, and that he is worthy of the honor which is bestowed on the greatest doctors of the Church, on Gregory and Ambrose, Augustine and Jerome; while others have not hesitated to propose St. Thomas for the exemplar and master of the academies and great lyceums, whom they may follow with unfaltering feet. On which point the words of Blessed Urban V to the Academy of Toulouse are worthy to recall: "It is our will, which we hereby enjoin upon you, that you follow the teaching of Blessed Thomas as the true and Catholic doctrine, and that you labor with all your force to profit by the same."[34] Innocent XII in the Letter in the form of a Brief addressed on February 6, 1694, to the University of Louvain, followed the example of Urban in the case of the University of Louvain, and Benedict XIV in the Letter in the form of a Brief addressed on August 26, 1752, to the Dionysian College of Granada; while to these judgments of great Pontiffs on Thomas Aquinas comes the crowning testimony of Innocent VI: "His teaching above that of others, the canons alone excepted, enjoys such an elegance of phraseology, a method of statement, a truth of proposition, that those who hold to it are never found swerving from the path of truth, and he who dare assail it will always be suspected of error."[35]

The ecumenical councils also, where blossoms the flower of all earthly wisdom, have always been careful to hold Thomas Aquinas in singular honor. In the councils of Lyons, Vienne, Florence, and the Vatican one might almost say that Thomas took part and presided over the deliberations and decrees of the Fathers, contending against the errors of the Greeks, of heretics and rationalists, with invincible force and with the happiest results. But the chief and special glory of Thomas, one which he has shared with none of the Catholic doctors, is that the Fathers of Trent made it part of the order of the conclave to lay upon the altar, together with the code of Sacred Scripture and the decrees of the Supreme Pontiffs, the *Summa* of Thomas Aquinas, whence to seek counsel, reason, and inspiration.

A last triumph was reserved for this incomparable man —namely, to compel the homage, praise, and admiration of even the very enemies of the Catholic name. For it has come to light that there were not lacking among the leaders of heretical sects some who openly declared that, if the teaching of Thomas Aquinas were only taken away, they could easily battle with all Catholic teachers, gain the victory, and abolish the Church.[36] A vain hope indeed, but no vain testimony.

Therefore, venerable brethren, as often as we contemplate the good, the force, and the singular advantages to be derived from this system of philosophy which our Fathers so dearly loved, we think it hazardous that its special honor should not always and everywhere remain, especially when it is established that daily experience, and the judgment of the greatest men, and, to crown all, the voice of the Church, have favored the scholastic philosophy. Moreover, to the old teaching a novel system of philosophy has succeeded here and there, in which we fail to perceive those desirable and wholesome fruits which the Church and civil society itself would prefer. For it pleased the struggling innovators of the sixteenth century to philosophize without any respect for faith, the power of inventing in accordance with his own pleasure and bent being asked and given in turn by each one. Hence it was natural that systems of philosophy multiplied beyond measure, and conclusions differing and clashing one with another arose even about those matters which are the most im-

17

portant in human knowledge. From a mass of conclusions men often come to wavering and doubt; and who knows not how easily the mind slips from doubt to error? But as men are apt to follow the lead given them, this new pursuit seems to have caught the souls of certain Catholic philosophers, who, throwing aside the patrimony of ancient wisdom, chose rather to build up a new edifice than to strengthen and complete the old by the aid of the new—ill advisedly, in sooth, and not without detriment to the sciences. For a multiform system of this kind, which depends on the authority and choice of any professor, has a foundation open to change, and consequently gives us a philosophy not firm and stable and robust like that of old, but tottering and feeble. And if perchance it sometimes finds itself scarcely equal to sustain the shock of its foes, it should recognize that the cause and the blame lie in itself. In saying this we have no intention of discountenancing the learned and able men who bring their industry and erudition, and, what is more, the wealth of new discoveries, to the service of philosophy; for, of course, we understand that this tends to the development of learning. But one should be very careful lest all or his chief labor be exhausted in these pursuits and in mere erudition. And the same thing is true of sacred theology, which, indeed, may be assisted and illustrated by all kinds of erudition, though it is absolutely necessary to approach it in the grave manner of the scholastics, in order that, the forces of revelation and reason being united in it, it may continue to be "the invincible bulwark of the faith."[37]

With wise forethought, therefore, not a few of the advocates of philosophical studies, when turning their minds recently to the practical reform of philosophy, aimed and aim at restoring the renowned teaching of Thomas Aquinas and winning it back to its ancient beauty.

We have learned with great joy that many members of your order, venerable brethren, have taken this plan to heart; and while we earnestly commend their efforts, we exhort them to hold fast to their purpose, and remind each and all of you that our first and most cherished idea is that you should all furnish a generous and copious supply to studious youth of those crystal rills of wisdom flowing in a never-ending and fertilizing stream from the fountainhead of the Angelic Doctor.

Many are the reasons why we are so desirous of this. In the first place, then, since in the tempest that is on us the Christian faith is being constantly assailed by the machinations and craft of a certain false wisdom, all youths, but especially those who are the growing hope of the Church, should be nourished on the strong and robust food of doctrine, that so, mighty in strength and armed at all points, they may become habituated to advance the cause of religion with force and judgment, *being ready always*, according to the apostolic counsel, *to satisfy every one that asks you a reason of that hope which is in you*,[38] and that they may be able to exhort in sound doctrine and to convince the gainsayers.[39] Many of those who, with minds alienated from the faith, hate Catholic institutions, claim reason as their sole mistress and guide. Now, we think that, apart from the supernatural help of God, nothing is better calculated to heal those minds and to bring them into favor with the Catholic faith than the solid doctrine of the Fathers and the scholastics, who so clearly and forcibly demonstrate the firm foundations of the faith, its divine origin, its certain truth, the arguments that sustain it, the benefits it has conferred on the human race, and its perfect accord with reason, in a manner to satisfy completely minds open to persuasion, however unwilling and repugnant.

Domestic and civil society even, which, as all see, is exposed to great danger from this plague of perverse opinions, would certainly enjoy a far more peaceful and secure existence if a more wholesome doctrine were taught in the academies and schools—one more in conformity with the teaching of the Church, such as is contained in the works of Thomas Aquinas.

For the teachings of Thomas on the true meaning of liberty, which at this time is running into license, on the divine origin of all authority, on laws and their force, on the paternal and just rule of princes, on obedience to the higher powers, on mutual charity one towards another—on all of these and kindred subjects have very great and invincible force to overturn those principles of the new order which are well known to be dangerous to the peaceful order of things and to public safety. In short, all studies ought to find hope of advancement and promise of assistance in this restoration of philosophic discipline which we have proposed. The arts were wont to draw from philosophy, as from a wise mistress, sound judgment and right method, and from it also their spirit as from the common fount of life. When philosophy stood stainless in honor and wise in judgment, then, as facts and constant experience showed, the liberal arts flourished as never before or since; but, neglected and almost blotted out, they lay prone since philosophy began to lean to error and join hands with folly. Nor will the physical sciences, which are now in such great repute, and by the renown of so many inventions draw such universal admiration to themselves, suffer detriment but find very great assistance in the re-establishment of the ancient philosophy. For the investigation of facts and the contemplation of nature is not alone sufficient for their profitable exercise and advance; but when facts have been established it is necessary to rise and apply ourselves to the study of the nature of corporeal things, to inquire into the laws which govern them and the principles whence their order and varied unity and mutual attraction in diversity arise. To such investigations it is wonderful what force and light and aid the scholastic philosophy, if judiciously taught, would bring.

And here it is well to note that our philosophy can only by the grossest injustice be accused of being opposed to the advance and development of natural science. For when the scholastics, following the opinion of the holy Fathers, always held in anthropology that the human intelligence is led to the knowledge of things without body and matter only by things sensible, they readily understood that nothing was of greater use to the philosopher than diligently to search into the mysteries of nature and to be devoted with assiduous patience to the study of physical things. And this they confirmed by their own example; for St. Thomas, Blessed Albertus Magnus, and other leaders of the scholastics were never so wholly rapt in the study of philosophy as not to give large attention to the knowledge of natural things; and, indeed, the number of their sayings and writings on these subjects, which recent professors approve of and admit to harmonize with truth, is by no means small. Moreover, in this very age many illustrious professors of the physical sciences openly testify that between certain and accepted conclusions of modern physics and the philosophic principles of the schools there is no conflict worthy of the name.

While, therefore, we hold that every word of wisdom, every useful thing by whomsoever discovered or planned, ought to be received with a willing and grateful mind, we exhort you, venerable brethren, in all earnestness to restore the golden wisdom of St. Thomas, and to spread it far and wide for the defense and beauty of the Catholic faith, for the good of society, and for the advantage of all the sciences. The wisdom of St. Thomas, we say; for if anything is taken up with too great subtlety by the scholastic doctors, or too carelessly stated—if there be anything that ill agrees with the discoveries of a later age, or, in a word, improbable in whatever way, it does not enter our mind to propose that for imitation to our age. Let carefully selected teachers endeavor to implant the doctrine of Thomas Aquinas in the minds of the students, and set forth clearly his solidity and excellence over others. Let the academies already founded or to be founded by you illustrate and defend this doctrine, and use it for the refutation of prevailing errors. But, lest the false for the true, or the corrupt for the pure be drunk in, be watchful that the doctrine of Thomas be drawn from his own fountains, or at least from those rivulets which, derived from the very fount, have thus far flowed, according to the established agreement of learned men, pure and clear; be careful to guard the minds of youth from those which are said to flow thence, but in reality are gathered from strange and unwholesome streams.

But well do we know that vain will be our efforts unless, venerable brethren, He helps our common cause who, in the words of divine Scripture, is called the God of all knowledge[40]; by which we are also admonished that *every best gift and every perfect gift is from above, coming down from the Father of lights*[41]; and again: *If any of you want wisdom, let him ask of God, who gives to all men abundantly, and upbraids not; and it shall be given him.*[42]

Therefore in this also let us follow the example of the Angelic Doctor, who never gave himself to reading or writing without first begging the blessing of God; who modestly confessed that whatever he knew he had aquired not so much by his own study and labor as by the divine gift. And therefore let us all, in humble and united prayer, beseech God to send forth the spirit of knowledge and of understanding to the children of the Church, and open their senses for the understanding of wisdom. And that we may receive fuller fruits of the divine goodness, offer up to God the most efficacious patronage of the Blessed Virgin Mary, who is called the seat of wisdom; having at the same time as advocates St. Joseph, the most chaste spouse of the Virgin, and Peter and Paul, the chiefs of the apostles, whose truth renewed the earth, which had fallen under the impure blight of error, filling it with the light of heavenly wisdom.

In fine, relying on the divine assistance and confiding in your pastoral zeal, we bestow on all of you, venerable brethren, on all the clergy and the flocks committed to your charge, the apostolic benediction as a pledge of heavenly gifts and a token of our special esteem.

1. Matthew 28:19.
2. Colossians 2:8.
3. 1 Corinthians 2:4.
4. *De Trin.*, xiv, I, 3 (PL 42, 1037).
5. Clem. Alex., *Strom.*, I, 16; VII, 3 (PG 8, 795; 9, 426).
6. Origen, *Epistola ad Gregorium* (PG 11, 87-91).
7. Clem. Alex., *Strom.*, I, 5 (PG 8, 718-719).
8. Romans 1:20.
9. *Ibid.*, 2:14, 15.
10. *Orat. paneg. ad Origen*, 14 (PG 10, 1094).
11. *Carm.* i, Iamb. 3.
12. *Vita Moysis* (PG 44, 359).
13. *Epist. ad Magnum*, 4 (PL 22, 667).
14. *De Doctr. Christ.*, I, ii, 40 (PL 34, 63).
15. Wisdom 13:1.
16. *Ibid.*, 13:5.
17. 2 Peter 1:16.
18. *Const. Dogm. de Fid. Cath.*, c. 3.
19. *Const. cit.*, c. 4.
20. *Loc. cit.*
21. *Strom.*, I, 20 (PG 8, 818).
22. *Epist. ad Magnum*, 2 (PL 22, 666).
23. Bulla *Apostolici regiminis*.
24. *Epist. 143 (al. 7), ad Marcelin.*, 7 (PL 33, 589).
25. *Const. Dogm. de Fid. Cath.*, c. 4.

26. 1 Corinthians 1:24.
27. Colossians 2:3.
28. *Epist. ad Magnum*, 4 (PL 22, 667).
29. *Loc. cit.*
30. *Apologet.* 46 (PL 1, 573).
31. *Inst.* vii, 7 (PL 6, 759).
32. Bulla *Triumphantis* an. 1588.
33. *In 2m. 2ae.*, q. 148, a. 4; Leonine ed. Vol. X, n. 6, p. 174.
34. *Const.* 5a. dat. die Aug. 3, 1368 ad Concell. Univ. Tolo.
35. *Serm. de S. Thoma.*
36. Bucer.
37. Sixtus V. Bulla *Triumphantis.*
38. 1 Peter 3:15.
39. Tit. 1:9.
40. 1 Kings 2:3.
41. Jas. 1:17.
42. Jas. 1:5.

Pauline *BOOKS & MEDIA*

ALASKA
750 West 5th Ave., Anchorage, AK 99501; 907-272-8183

CALIFORNIA
3908 Sepulveda Blvd., Culver City, CA 90230; 310-397-8676
5945 Balboa Ave., San Diego, CA 92111; 619-565-9181
46 Geary Street, San Francisco, CA 94108; 415-781-5180

FLORIDA
145 S.W. 107th Ave., Miami, FL 33174; 305-559-6715

HAWAII
1143 Bishop Street, Honolulu, HI 96813; 808-521-2731

ILLINOIS
172 North Michigan Ave., Chicago, IL 60601; 312-346-4228

LOUISIANA
4403 Veterans Memorial Blvd., Metairie, LA 70006; 504-887-7631

MASSACHUSETTS
50 St. Paul's Ave., Jamaica Plain, Boston, MA 02130; 617-522-8911
Rte. 1, 885 Providence Hwy., Dedham, MA 02026; 617-326-5385

MISSOURI
9804 Watson Rd., St. Louis, MO 63126; 314-965-3512

NEW JERSEY
561 U.S. Route 1, Wick Plaza, Edison, NJ 08817; 908-572-1200

NEW YORK
150 East 52nd Street, New York, NY 10022; 212-754-1110
78 Fort Place, Staten Island, NY 10301; 718-447-5071

OHIO
2105 Ontario Street, Cleveland, OH 44115; 216-621-9427

PENNSYLVANIA
9171-A Roosevelt Blvd., Philadelphia, PA
19114; 215-676-9494

SOUTH CAROLINA
243 King Street, Charleston, SC 29401; 803-577-0175

TENNESSEE
4811 Poplar Ave., Memphis, TN 38117; 901-761-2987

TEXAS
114 Main Plaza, San Antonio, TX 78205; 210-224-8101

VIRGINIA
1025 King Street, Alexandria, VA 22314; 703-549-3806

CANADA
3022 Dufferin Street, Toronto, Ontario, Canada M6B 3T5; 416-781-9131
1155 Yonge Street, Toronto, Ontario, Canada M4T 1W2; 416-934-3440